Choice
Edmund Newell

DARTON·LONGMAN+TODD

First published in 2012 by
Darton, Longman and Todd Ltd
1 Spencer Court
140 – 142 Wandsworth High Street
London SW18 4JJ

© 2012 Edmund Newell

The right of Edmund Newell to be identified as the author of this work has been asserted in accordance with the Copyright, Designs and Patents Act 1998.

ISBN: 978-0-232-52887-9

A catalogue record for this book is available from the British Library.

Phototypeset by Judy Linard
Printed and bound by GZ Digital Media

Contents

1. *Dear Diary* — 5
2. *Choices, Choices…* — 7
3. *'The Better Part'* — 9
4. *Too Much Choice?* — 11
5. *Choice and Freedom* — 14
6. *Coping with Choice* — 17
7. *Narrowing Down Choices* — 21
8. *'Slaves of Righteousness'* — 24
9. *What Would Jesus Do?* — 28
10. *Poor Choices* — 32
11. *Ethics and Choice* — 35
12. *Setting the Moral Compass* — 42
13. *Ethics and Consumer Choice* — 45
14. *Choose life!* — 48
15. *Postscript: Religion and Rational Choice* — 52
    Suggestions for Further Reading — 56

1
Dear Diary

Unexpectedly warm and sunny this morning, so celebrate by switching to summer clothing. Tea and toast for breakfast - can't face muesli again! Given the weather, decide to leave car at home and cycle to work - good for the environment (not to mention the waistline...).

Spend most of the morning interviewing for a new receptionist - an almost impossible task as all the candidates are excellent. The person we offered the post to wants 24 hours to think about it, as she has another job offer. Interviews overran into lunchtime, so grabbed an inedible sandwich and remembered just in time to buy Gran a birthday card. Hope she can cope with the puppies - it was that or a risqué joke.

Difficult afternoon in the office deciding on further budget cuts - we've already trimmed things to the bone. No difficulty though in replying 'No thanks' - again! - to Pete's text asking me out for a drink after work. Can't he take a hint that it's over?! Reminds me - call Dave.

Cycle home in the rain and get drenched. Must remember to check weather forecast next time!

CHOICE

Quick trip to the supermarket turns into a marathon – why do they keep moving things around so you can't find them, and how am I supposed to choose between fifty types of coffee?! Relieved to get home and eat in front of the telly, but after channel hopping decide to read a book instead – the one Dave recommended. Thanks Dave – good choice!

Spend time thinking and praying about tomorrow – must decide whether to go to the church council meeting or a colleague's farewell party – should really be at both.

2
Choices, choices ...

AS OUR DIARIST reminds us, each and every day we are confronted with choices. Some may be straightforward and involve quick decisions, such as what to have for breakfast or what clothes to wear. Others may be complex and involve long deliberation, such as who to employ or how to handle budgets at home or at work. The consequences of our choices may be of little importance: we may get wet if we choose to cycle to work. Or they may be life-changing: the friends we choose (and those who choose us) may determine who we will spend the rest of our lives with.

Day in, day out, we are faced with choices and have decisions to make where we must weigh up options. At the time we make a decision it is hard to know what the impact might be. What at first may seem trivial may prove to be significant, whereas those things we judge as important may prove of little consequence. What is for sure, though, is that the choices we make will shape our lives and the lives of others: whether it's the cumulative effect of many small choices that expresses so much about who we are and what our attitudes are, or whether it's the choices we make when major, life-changing decisions have to be taken.

CHOICE

How, then, do we decide what to choose? There will be many factors at play, including our mood, upbringing, education, opinions and beliefs. The purpose of this book is to explore the latter: how we make choices, and in particular how having a Christian faith might inform the decisions we make. Following Jesus is itself an ongoing matter of choice, and so reflecting on how we came to that decision and how our religious commitment is sustained may help us to better understand ourselves and inform the other choices we make as we seek to live our lives as Christian disciples.

3
'The Better Part'

THERE IS A WONDERFUL story about choice and discipleship in Luke's gospel: the story of Jesus visiting the home of Martha and Mary:

> Now as they went on their way, he entered a certain village, where a woman named Martha welcomed him into her home. She had a sister named Mary, who sat at the Lord's feet and listened to what he was saying. But Martha was distracted by her many tasks; so she came to him and asked, 'Lord, do you not care that my sister has left me to do all the work by myself? Tell her then to help me.' But the Lord answered her, 'Martha, Martha, you are worried and distracted by many things; there is need of only one thing. Mary has chosen the better part, which will not be taken away from her.' (Luke 10: 38-42)

When Jesus arrives at their home, Martha and Mary must decide what to do. Martha chooses to work – perhaps to prepare a meal for their guest – while her sister Mary chooses to sit at Jesus' feet and listen to him. According to Jesus, it's Mary who has 'chosen the better part'. Poor hard-working Martha! She has opted to be a hostess, making her guest welcome. Mary, on the other hand, has chosen to be a disciple.

The point of the story is not to put Martha down, but to play up Mary's choice of discipleship. Martha's choice was good; Mary's was better. The story has impact because we can empathise with Martha: we might well do the same if we were in her situation. Yet if we choose 'the better part' – to be a disciple of Jesus – this will be life-changing and, hopefully, life-enhancing. Indeed, it will have such an influence that it will inform the choices we make in all aspects of our lives. Choice, then, is a matter of faith.

FOR REFLECTION
Consider your own journey of faith. What have been the influences on that journey? What major decisions have you taken in response to your faith?

4
Too Much Choice?

THOMAS HOBSON WAS a livery stable owner in Cambridge, who lived from 1544 to 1631. It is said that to ensure all his forty or so horses were used regularly he gave his customers the choice of hiring the horse in the stall nearest the door or no horse at all, hence the term 'Hobson's choice'.

What would Thomas Hobson make of life in the twenty-first century? He would probably be amazed at the amount of choice many of us face. A consequence of our society's relative affluence, the communications revolution and the opening-up of global markets is that we are confronted with a greater range of goods and services to choose from than ever before. As a result, we have more decisions to make. For example, for those of us of a certain age, watching television used to be a matter almost of Hobson's choice: it was BBC, ITV, or the off button. Then we got BBC1 and BBC2. Later there was Channel 4, followed by Channel 5. Now in Britain, if we choose to have the right equipment, there is a bamboozling selection of 530 TV channels, from Aastha – The Faith Station to Zone Reality Extra. At times, such a range of choice can seem so overwhelming that it is no wonder that our diarist turned off the television and read a book instead.

As our diarist observed, a trip to the supermarket can also be bewildering. According to the Food Marketing Institute, the average American supermarket has a range of 48,750 goods – five times as many as in 1975. However, our diarist got it wrong about coffee. At the time of writing, Tesco online offers a choice of not 50 but 228 coffee products. Not so long ago asking for a cup of coffee in a café involved deciding whether or not to have milk and sugar. Nowadays, it may require working out whether to have a latte, cappuccino, espresso or mocha, or some variant of these; whether it's tall, grande, or venti; whether the milk is full-fat, half-fat or skinny; whether the coffee is caffeinated or 'no fun'; whether or not to have syrup, and if so what flavour; whether it is hot or on ice; and whether to have a chocolate or cinnamon topping – by which time we may have lost the will to live, let alone to have a drink.

Making good choices in the face of having so much to choose from can be problematic. The bewildering range of choice to which many of us are now exposed is attracting the attention of psychologists and behavioural scientists. A leading figure in this area, Barry Schwartz, argues in his book *The Paradox of Choice* that consumers reach a point when the effort required to make a choice between so many options outweighs the benefits of variety, such that the process of choosing becomes debilitating. This view is supported by a growing body of research.

In a pioneering experiment conducted in a Californian grocery store, shoppers were offered 24 jams to taste, and were given a discount voucher to buy any of the jams in the store afterwards. The experiment was repeated another day, but this time with only 6 jams on offer. While the display of 24 jams attracted more shoppers than the display of 6 jams, only 3 percent of those who stopped at the larger display went on to buy some jam, as opposed to 30 per cent of those who stopped at the 6 jam display. Similar results have been found with a range of other experiments, which all point to the demotivating effect of having too much to choose from – not something that Thomas Hobson's customers complained of!

FOR REFLECTION
How do you feel when you face a large amount of choice, say in a supermarket? Have you ever felt that you were being offered too much choice? How do you decide what to choose in such a situation?

5
Choice and Freedom

This negative view of choice is a relatively new phenomenon and is associated with our rapidly changing world and lifestyles. It is certainly in contrast to how choice is normally perceived, which is as an expression of freedom and therefore highly desirable.

Both extending the choices available to as many people as possible and having the freedom to choose are normally regarded as signs of a healthy society. This is true not only for consumers. Freedom of choice has long been an aspiration associated with democracy. The ability to choose political leaders and representatives without coercion is seen by many as a fundamental human right and necessary for good governance. Choice has also become important in the field of healthcare. When the National Health Service was established in 1948, patients had little to choose from in terms of the care they received. More recently, and especially since 2007, patient choice has come to the fore in health policy. Today patients have the right to choose their GP surgery, which hospital to go to for treatment, the consultant they see, and the type of care they receive.

Within the field of economics choice is seen positively across the political spectrum, and this has major policy implications. For decades, the controversial economist Milton Friedman extolled the virtues of choice and free markets and famously influenced Ronald Reagan and Margaret Thatcher. In 1980 Friedman expounded his views to millions of viewers in a ten-part television series called *Free to Choose*. Another Nobel Prize-winning economist, Amartya Sen, much of whose work focuses on championing the cause of the poorest of the poor, also regards choice as being of fundamental importance. In his book *Development as Freedom*, Sen writes of a core objective of development as being to enhance 'people's capability to choose the lives they have reason to value.'[1]

While choice undoubtedly enables markets to work efficiently and offers us an important way to exercise our freedom and to benefit from the things that become available to us, a question we must now face is whether rather than being liberating, a high degree of choice actually stifles human flourishing. Certainly the growing body of research into happiness and well-being suggests that despite the increased affluence in western societies since the Second World War, many of us are no happier than we were in the 1950s, and in some respects our well-being may have actually decreased. The expanding range of choice could well be one factor in this, given the stress associated with making choices.

[1] Amartya Sen, *Development as Freedom* (Oxford: Oxford University Press, 2001) p. 63.

CHOICE

We cannot escape making choices, and the likelihood is that we will encounter more and more choice in many aspects of our lives - from things as trivial as buying greetings cards to as serious as deciding what treatment to receive for a life-threatening disease. Given this is the case, learning to choose well is becoming of ever-greater importance if we are to flourish and enjoy the freedom and opportunities available to us. So how do we choose well, and what has faith got to do with it?

FOR REFLECTION
What are the things that most influence our sense of happiness or well-being? Have these changed over time?

6
Coping with Choice

ARE WE HARD to please? The answer to this question may well point to how we are affected by an overwhelming amount of choice.

Research by Barry Schwartz and his colleagues suggests that those of us who are hard to please and always strive to make the best possible choice – those they call 'maximizers' – are likely to be those who struggle most with having too much to choose from. The reason is as follows. First of all, those of us who want to make the best choices are facing more and more decisions in our daily lives. When it comes to shopping around for the best deal or the item that most closely meets our needs, we inevitably research and compare products. The more there is to choose from, the more research and comparisons are involved. For maximizers, this can become an increasingly difficult and time-consuming task.

Then, when a choice has been made, those of us who are hard to please will be more likely to be dissatisfied with what we have chosen. This is because we are more likely to be aware of the value or 'opportunity cost' of the things we decide not to choose due to the research we have done. As a result, we are more likely to regret or be disappointed by the choices we make. In the worst case, Schwartz suggests that those of us who are maximizers may even become paralysed by the various options and unable to choose, which could contribute to causing depression.

If this is a depressing thought, then there is better news from the research. For those of us who are easier to please, choosing is more straightforward. At the opposite end of the spectrum to maximizers are those Schwartz and his colleagues call 'satisficers' – those of us who are more easily satisfied and make choices that are simply 'good enough' for what we want. Rather than spending time and energy seeking the best possible option, or freezing up when confronted by a wide range of choice, satisficers are more generally relaxed when it comes to choosing and more content with their decision, so long as it meets their basic needs.

Bearing all this in mind, Schwartz makes four suggestions for how to cope with excessive choice:

- First, when the choices we face are relatively unimportant, we should set limits on what to choose from. For instance, rather than go to every possible shop in search of something, we might restrict ourselves to a couple of shops.
- Second, if we are hard to please, we might work on becoming satisficers and train ourselves to not always seek the best option and to be content with what we have chosen.

- Third, we might also try to put out of our minds what we think we are missing out on by not having the things we did not choose.
- And finally, he advises us to control our expectations and not expect too much from what we choose, and learn to be satisfied with what we have chosen.

Although this research is focused on consumer choice, Schwartz's advice makes good sense when applied to other situations where we are confronted with a wide range of things to choose from. The key is to come up with practical strategies to reduce choice and to cultivate an attitude of being content with our decisions. Interestingly, Schwartz points out that this requires 'practice, discipline and perhaps a new way of thinking'.[2] There is resonance here with the techniques associated with Christian formation, and Christian teaching on the dangers of materialism is particularly pertinent when dealing with consumer choice. For those seeking to become less like maximizers and more like satisficers, it is worth reflecting on Jesus' teaching from the Sermon on the Mount:

You cannot serve God and wealth.

Therefore I tell you, do not worry about your life, what you will eat or what you will drink, or about

[2] Barry Schwartz, 'The Tyranny of Choice', *Scientific American*, April 2004, p.75

your body, what you will wear. Is not life more than food, and the body more than clothing? Look at the birds of the air; they neither sow nor reap nor gather into barns, and yet your heavenly Father feeds them. Are you not of more value than they? (Matthew 6:24-6)

FOR REFLECTION
When it comes to making choices, where would you place yourself on a spectrum with maximizers at one end and satisficers at the other?

7
Narrowing Down Choices

NAVIGATING THE COMPLEXITIES of choice is something that the writer and retreat leader Margaret Silf has also explored.[3] Like Schwartz, she too emphasises the importance of narrowing down what we choose from in order to make life less stressful. However, rather than set some arbitrary limits, such as the number of shops we visit, she suggests that there are four things we should consider that will help to make choosing manageable:

- Are the options realistic?
- Are they practically possible?
- Are they compatible with our current commitments and/or responsibilities?
- How do they sit with our conscience?

The first three points are sheer common sense. If any of the choices before us is unrealistic, practically impossible or incompatible with other aspects of our lives then we should lay such options aside and not let them distract us. A simple exercise of this kind will help to narrow our choices so we can focus on those options that are

[3] Margaret Silf, *On Making Choices*, (Oxford: Lion, 2004).

realistic, practically possible and workable given our obligations. This is not to say that the choices we discard should be forgotten. Something that is unrealistic now may well be possible in the future; but for the moment it is not relevant and so should be taken out of the equation.

Making choices can sometimes be a lonely business, but often decision-making can be shared with other people. When dealing with choice, it is clearly important to determine whether others should or could be involved in the process. Most relationships at home or at work are put to the test at some point when someone is left out when making a key decision.

Buying a house or a car may well be a family decision, for example. But when we are choosing where to live or spending a lot of money on something like a car it may also be helpful to seek the advice and support of someone with some relevant experience or expertise, both for peace of mind (*'caveat emptor'* – 'let the buyer beware') and also to make a well-informed decision. Even when choices are personal to ourselves, getting the objective advice of someone we trust, or using that person as a sounding-board to test our thoughts and ideas, can be helpful when it comes to considering the sort of questions Margaret Silf suggests we should address.

Silf's fourth point, however, takes the issue of making choices to another level. How our choices sit with our conscience means looking at the options through the lens of our moral values. Decision-making of this kind goes far beyond the practical concerns of making the choices that best suit our needs. Instead, it brings ethics and the needs of others into the equation. When moral questions are raised by the choices we face, it is here that faith may have a significant role to play. Much of the remainder of this book is therefore concerned with looking at choice from the perspective of Christian ethics.

FOR REFLECTION
What are the choices that you wish to make only by yourself? What choices would you make together with others? What choices that affect you are you content to leave for others to decide?

8
'Slaves of Righteousness'

WE HAVE ALREADY noted the close relationship between choice and freedom. The earliest Christian text on the meaning of freedom is Paul's Letter to the Romans. Written in the mid- to late-50s in the first century AD in preparation for a visit to the church in Rome, Paul begins by describing himself in a way that appears at first to speak of the opposite of freedom: 'Paul, a servant of Jesus Christ', or a more accurately translated, 'Paul, a *slave* of Jesus Christ'. (Romans 1:1)

The Letter to the Romans is notoriously difficult to get to grips with, but at its core Paul describes alternative ways of living: under the influence of sin and death, and under 'righteousness'. The latter, he argues, is the good life made possible by the death and resurrection of Jesus Christ, and baptism is the means by which we signify the move from one state to the other. For Paul, then, freedom is about the release from the destructive grip of sin and death to life under the influence of Jesus Christ, with the transition marked by baptism. The choice is ours.

The extent to which we have free will is a question that has exercised philosophers over the centuries, and more recently has become the subject of scientific research. At one extreme, the philosopher Descartes argued that we have total free will, echoing to a degree what Saint Augustine wrote centuries earlier in his treatise *On Free Choice of the Will*, which presupposes, like Paul, that the will is free to choose between good and evil. Others, observing the human propensity to act in certain pre-determined ways, have argued for various levels of 'determinism': that the will is to a greater or lesser degree conditioned by various factors (including perhaps genetic make-up) which shape our behaviour, including how we make choices. Just as, say, we might be hard or easy to please, so we might be predisposed to take or avoid risks when confronted with choice with different levels of risk – something which might affect the choices we make about saving money, for example. The truth is probably somewhere in the middle: that basically we have free will, but it is constrained in various ways by factors including personality-type and upbringing.

Returning to Paul, he is quick to point out that freedom from sin and death does not mean that Christians are free to do whatever they like. Some of the Christian community in Rome were Jewish Christians, and with these in mind Paul makes plain that while being baptised in Christ may mean that they are no longer bound by the Jewish law which regulated much of their daily life, it does not give them carte blanche to behave without any sort of moral code.

Christians should live in ways that respect the dignity of being baptised in Christ, for 'having been set free from sin', writes Paul, you 'have become slaves of righteousness' (Romans 6:18). What does this slavery entail? Amongst other things, it means living under an ethical code that is compatible with the teaching and example of Jesus Christ.

Paul points to a paradox. While it seems we are created with free will, it appears that God's will is for us to exercise that freedom in certain ways if we are to flourish. We have the option to choose to live in ways that take us down the route of sin and death, or we can choose the way of righteousness – which is where our true freedom lies. Freedom for the Christian disciple means spiritual liberation, not necessarily freedom in a worldly sense. It is the sort of freedom expressed beautifully in the Collect for Peace, which many Anglicans say regularly in the *Book of Common Prayer* Service of Morning Prayer:

> O God, who art the author of peace and lover of concord, in knowledge of whom standeth our eternal life, *whose service is perfect freedom*: Defend us thy humble servants in all assaults of our enemies; that we, surely trusting in thy defence, may not fear the power of any adversaries; through the might of Jesus Christ our Lord. Amen.

FOR REFLECTION

When making choices, are you ever aware of instinctive feelings that influence your decision-making? Have you ever had the experience where your reason is telling you to choose one thing, while emotionally you prefer another?

9
What Would Jesus Do?

THE 'GLOOMY DEAN' of St Paul's, London, Dean Inge, once said that 'Christianity promises to make men free; it never promises to make them independent.'[4] Being a disciple of Christ involves recognising our interdependence as members of the Body of Christ, and our obligations and responsibilities to one another. When it comes to making choices, ethics therefore play an important part of our decision-making.

Were he alive today, Dean Inge is probably not the sort of person who would wear a wristband with the letters 'WWJD?' which stand for 'What Would Jesus Do?' Whatever our church tradition, however, a benchmark for Christian ethical decision-making is 'what is the Christ-like thing to do?' This could be restated slightly differently in a way which might resonate with those of other faiths or none: 'what is the loving thing to do?'

Turning to the Bible for insight and guidance when it comes to making choices is a fundamental aspect of Christian discipleship. In the Hebrew Scriptures, or Old Testament, we can find wisdom gleaned over millennia

---

[4] W.R. Inge, *The Philosophy of Plotinus*, Volume 2 (London: Longmans, Green and Co., 1929), p. 192.

as people sought to live their lives as a response to God. For the Christian, the New Testament has much to say about discipleship.

Turning to the Bible for help in decision-making is not without its difficulties, however. Much of it relates to situations and cultures far removed from our own, and how scripture is understood and interpreted can be contentious and certainly requires care – hence the importance of biblical commentaries, bible study, and sermons.

From the point of view of this book, there is another issue to consider: Jesus sets the bar high when it comes to ethical standards. We can see this clearly in the most important collection of Jesus' teaching on ethics, the Sermon on the Mount in Matthew's gospel. On a number of occasions the refrain is used 'you have heard that it was said … but I say…', in which Jesus takes an ethical issue and gives a challenging interpretation. For instance, '"It was … said, 'Whoever divorces his wife, let him give her a certificate of divorce.' But I say to you that anyone who divorces his wife, except on the ground of unchastity, causes her to commit adultery; and whoever marries a divorced woman commits adultery."' (Matthew 5:31-2)

This passage deals with one of the most important decisions we are likely to make: whether or not to enter into a committed relationship. How we make such a choice goes far beyond the scope of this book, but there are some important points to consider in relation to what has been discussed so far.

First of all, the passage highlights the importance of handling scripture with care. What Jesus says can come across as being harsh from the perspective of our own times and culture, where marriages can fail for all sorts of reasons other than infidelity and where remarriage may be seen as the best outcome for families that have been broken-up by divorce. However, in its original context in a patriarchal society, Jesus' strict teaching on the grounds for divorce offered protection for women who would be left vulnerable if their marriage failed. The compassionate element of this teaching is easy to miss if taken out of context, and it begs the question 'what would Jesus do?' if he were speaking in the context of our contemporary society?

What is probably the case is that he would set high ethical standards to which to aspire. This was certainly true for his earliest followers. '"You have heard that it was said, 'You shall not commit adultery'", says Jesus earlier in the Sermon on the Mount, '"But I say to you that everyone who looks at a woman with lust has already committed adultery with her in his heart."' (Matthew 5:27-8) This passage highlights another difficulty we face when handling scripture. Here, Jesus uses hyperbole to show how we are to be freed from the destructive effects of infidelity, which can destroy our most important relationships. Jesus pushes the point to its extreme to show that what we have to deal with goes deep and may even go beyond our consciousness.

The intention of such teaching is to be liberating and life-enhancing, not guilt-inducing and stifling. Nevertheless, many religions – not least certain expressions of Christianity – have a reputation for the latter. As these examples from the Sermon on the Mount highlight, this is particularly relevant to choices concerning relationships. A failed marriage or relationship, for whatever reason, is likely to cause difficulties for those whose religious tradition places an emphasis on life-long commitment. The fear of making the wrong choice of partner can also cause problems for those setting out in relationships. 'Is this the person I really want to spend the rest of my life with?' is an important question for a person in his or her twenties in an age where average life expectancy in Britain is rapidly working its way towards one hundred.

FOR REFLECTION
Are there times when you turn to the Bible for guidance when making decisions? If so, in what ways do you make use of the scriptures?

10
Poor Choices

DESPITE OUR BEST efforts not to, from time to time we will make poor choices. We might realise immediately that we have chosen badly, or our choices may prove to be wrong further down the line. This book is partly about how to choose well and so minimize the possibility of making poor choices. Nevertheless, it will still happen. So how do we deal with this?

What is important here, and just mentioned with regard to relationships, is our attitude to failure. If we are afraid of failing, particularly if we set ourselves high ethical or other standards, we will be fearful of making bad choices. In fact, we will be fearful of making choices *per se*, dreading decisions in case we get them wrong. As a result, we might become indecisive, vacillating between options. Worse still, like the 'maximizers' mentioned earlier, we might be paralysed by the fear of getting things wrong. If, however, our approach to life is more relaxed, and our attitude to failure is that it presents opportunities to learn from our mistakes, then making wrong choices can become an important aspect of personal growth and development.

Learning from failures is certainly an aspect of maturing in Christian discipleship, and the New Testament provides many insights into how our human frailties are perceived by God. Famously, in the story of his encounter with the woman caught in adultery and threatened with execution by stoning, Jesus chooses not to condemn her for her actions (John 7:53–8:11). This story not only gives us insight into forgiveness, but of the potential to learn from, and grow as a result of, the mistakes we make.

If Jesus sets an example of high ethical standards for us to aspire to, then throughout the gospels his disciples offer us a different sort of role model. As well as being people who respond positively to Jesus' call to follow him, time and time again they are portrayed as flawed human beings who learn important lessons through their misunderstandings and failures along the way. What we see in the gospels, and what is confirmed in the Acts of the Apostles, is that the disciples grow in stature as they learn from Jesus and from their experiences as his followers. Simon Peter, in particular, is the disciple who exemplifies learning through failure.

Like Mary, Simon Peter chooses 'the better part' to follow Jesus, and gives up his career as a fisherman. What his family make of this choice we are not told. However, what soon becomes clear is that Simon Peter does not fully understand what Christian discipleship entails or means. Here is a disciple who learns from his mistakes, many of which stem from his over-enthusiasm.

It is Simon Peter who jumps into the water to go to Jesus who he sees walking on the water, and nearly drowns trying to meet him. Simon Peter is one of the disciples who accompanies Jesus to the Garden of Gethsemane after the Last Supper, and is the one whom Jesus upbraids for being unable to keep awake. It is Simon Peter who tells Jesus 'I will never desert you', but after Jesus' arrest denies him three times. Yet it is Simon Peter who is forgiven by the risen Christ, who is given the name Peter, which means 'rock', by Jesus and told 'you are Peter, and on this rock I will build my church' (Matthew 16:18).

The image of Peter in the New Testament is certainly not of someone who is paralysed by the fear of getting things wrong – quite the reverse. The gospel writers use stories about Jesus' disciples to provide encouragement for other followers of Christ, and Peter is the archetype for Christian discipleship. The enthusiastic but error-prone Peter learns from his mistakes, including what it is to be forgiven and having the opportunity to start afresh, and the Acts of the Apostles presents him as someone who made the best of this opportunity as one of the key missionaries of early Christianity. When Jesus chose Peter as 'the rock', he chose well.

Perhaps, then, an alternative wristband to the one with 'WWJD?' for those struggling to make sense of their faith and to put it into practice could be 'WWPD?' – 'What Would Peter Do?'

FOR REFLECTION
What are the mistakes you have made from which you feel you have learned most?

11
Ethics and Choice

THE GREAT VIOLINIST Yehudi Menuhin made a connection between discipline and freedom in his book *Themes and Variations*. 'The price of freedom for all musicians, both composers and interpreters, is tremendous control, discipline and patience,' he wrote, 'but perhaps not only for musicians. Do we not all find freedom to improvise, in all art, in all life, along the guiding lines of discipline?'[5] What is being suggested in this book is that making good choices is about using our free will in a disciplined way shaped by faith. But what are the 'guiding lines' to help us make 'good' choices in an ethical sense?

In practice, the moral choices that we make – what we reckon to be right or wrong, good or bad, desirable or undesirable – are rarely done with logical precision. Instead, we draw on a mixture of experience, views, convictions, beliefs and personality traits to guide us. How much weight we might place on any of these at any given time might depend on our mood or circumstance. So how can we approach making good choices in a disciplined manner? A useful place to start is to

[5] Yehudi Menuhin, *Themes and Variations* (London, Heinemann, 1972), p.46.

consider the various schools of thought on moral philosophy. Here we can discover the theory behind the ethics that can be applied to the choices we make.

Over the centuries, moral philosophy – Christian or otherwise – has focused on three areas:

- Are there fundamental moral rules governing the duties we have towards each other?
- What are the moral consequences of our actions?
- Are there characteristics that promote good behaviour, and if so how can they be encouraged and developed?

To use the terminology of moral philosophy, these can be categorised as: deontological, consequentialist, and virtue ethics. Religiously-based ethics tend to focus on the former and latter: moral rules and duties that we should always follow, and the type of character we should seek to develop. In both cases, the Bible has proved highly influential, as Jesus' teachings and other ethical texts have helped shape the thinking of some of the great minds over the centuries.

So how can these different approaches to ethics help us deal with the choices we face? Before answering that question, it is worth looking more closely at each approach, and how they can be used in decision-making.

ETHICS AND CHOICE

Duties

Deontological ethics gets its name from the Greek word for duty, *deos*, and is based on the view that there are universal moral principles or 'duties' that should govern our behaviour. Those who hold this view believe it is possible to discern things that are clearly right or wrong – moral absolutes – and other moral imperatives that lead to living a good life. Examples of moral absolutes are not to kill, torture or deliberately harm people, and examples of moral imperatives are treating people fairly and with honesty, and loving our neighbours as ourselves.

Deontological ethics is rooted in the concept of 'natural law'. Natural law is grounded in both classical philosophy and theology, which share the view that there is a moral code embedded within the universe which has been divinely revealed and which human reason and thought can access. Natural law is particularly associated with the Greek philosopher Aristotle, who believed there is a universal moral code that governs what leading a 'good life' entails, and also to the thirteenth-century Christian theologian and philosopher Thomas Aquinas. The idea of natural law is also found in the Wisdom literature of the Hebrew Scriptures, and its earliest expression in the Christian tradition is in the Letter to the Romans, where Paul writes of what is required for a Christian to live a good life being 'written on their hearts, to which their own conscience also bears witness'. (Romans 2:15).

Others who have shared the view of there being common moral principles deeply ingrained within human nature, but from a non-religious perspective, include the philosophers John Locke, who championed the notion of there being universal human rights, and Immanuel Kant, who argued that our duties towards each other can be worked out by human reason alone.

Kant put forward the view that there is a 'categorical imperative' that should shape the way we behave. He expressed this in various ways, one of which is 'Act in such a way that you always treat humanity, whether in your own person or in the person of any other, never simply as a means, but always at the same time as an end.' There is a strong resonance between Kant's categorical imperative and the 'Golden Rule', the ancient ethical principle shared by most religions and cultures and famously expressed in Christianity by Jesus as 'In everything do to others as you would have them do to you'. (Matthew 7:12). The universality of the Golden Rule supports the idea of natural law – that certain moral principles are deeply ingrained in us and shared across humanity.

Consequences

Consequentialist ethics focuses on outcomes rather than moral duties. Those who advocate this approach emphasise the importance of trying to assess the best or most desirable result when making a decision.

ETHICS AND CHOICE

Among consequentialist thinkers are Thomas Hobbes, who believed that human nature is fundamentally self-interested and that we should act in ways that maximise our own long-term interests. The most influential form of consequentialist ethics, however, is utilitarianism, and anyone who has studied economics at school or university will understand its significance. The basic principle of utilitarianism is that we should act in ways that seek to maximise the good, happiness, pleasure, or 'utility' of the greatest number of people. Associated in particular with Jeremy Bentham and John Stuart Mill, as students of economics will know, utilitarianism provides the underlying ethics underpinning of much economic theory.

At first sight, aiming to make as many people as possible happy seems a laudable goal. However, utilitarianism has proved controversial and is riddled with difficulties. What is 'utility' and how should it be measured? How can we reliably assess the likely consequences of our actions? What happens when there are multiple consequences to consider, and how do we weigh them up together? Should outcomes, however desirable, take priority over other ethical considerations?

Despite the questions and difficulties, consequentialism is rightly an important branch of ethics. Assessing possible outcomes is essential to decision-making, and can be a powerful ally when working alongside other forms of moral reasoning.

Virtues

With ancient roots in the writings of the Greek philosopher Plato, and further developed in the Middle Ages by Thomas Aquinas, virtue ethics is based on the understanding that there are desirable human traits or characteristics that naturally work to promote that which is good – the 'disposition to act well', to quote Aquinas. Virtue ethics has undergone something of a renaissance in recent years, perhaps in response to what are regarded as less than desirable influences in society at large, including greed, cynicism, individualism and materialism.

Courage, temperance, prudence and justice – these are the 'cardinal' or 'natural' or key virtues that should be nurtured. These virtues are easily misunderstood. Temperance is not about abstaining from drinking alcohol, for example. Instead, what is meant is that our behaviour should be tempered by reason rather than emotion or instinct. Likewise, prudence does not refer to being careful with money, but means being prudential in our reasoning – having the capacity to make wise ethical decisions. Courage and justice refer to what we would normally associate them with, however.

While deontological and consequentialist ethics are about our actions, virtue ethics is about the sort of people we are, since our character heavily influences our behaviour. However, our behaviour also influences our character, and reflecting on the consequences of our behaviour is character-building. So virtue ethics sits alongside other ethical schools of thought, providing an important complementary component to our moral compass. Indeed, if our character makes us more likely to think about ethics, we are more likely to consider our duties to others and possible moral consequences when making our choices.

FOR REFLECTION
What, if any, are the moral absolutes that you would not be prepared to compromise when making an ethical decision?

12
Setting the Moral Compass

HOW WE MAKE sense of different approaches to ethics is something that has been explored by the philosopher Alasdair MacIntyre, who is critical of the way ethics is often put into practice.[6] In particular, he is concerned with 'moral relativism' – of seeing ethics as a product of our culture rather than of universal moral principles. If our ethics are regarded as being moulded by cultural values rather than by any universal moral code, then this can encourage us to rationalise what we *want* to do, rather than to consider what we *ought* to do – just as there is a temptation to trawl the Bible for a text, taken out of context, to justify something we have said or done.

Moral relativism often sits uncomfortably with religion. From a Christian perspective – and one shared by many other faiths and philosophies – there are clear moral principles that should be followed in all walks of life. Perhaps the most obvious example is the Ten Commandments, which lay down some basic ethical principles for Jews and Christians alike. Similarly, Jesus' teaching on love, such as his challenging

[6] Alasdair MacIntyre, *After Virtue: A Study in Moral Theory*, 3rd revised edn (London: Duckworth, 2007)

injunction in the Sermon on the Mount, 'But I say to you, love your enemies and pray for those who persecute you' (Matthew 5:44), provides some clear ethical guidelines.

However, we may well face situations where moral absolutes or imperatives are unable to guide us to the point of making a decision. Considering the likely consequences of how we might choose to act could then become key, while our thinking more generally will be shaped by our character. Bearing this in mind, we are likely to draw upon deontological, consequentialist, and virtue ethics when making our moral choices. If this is done in a reasoned way it avoids the trap of moral relativism, because it sees these different approaches as complementary rather than as alternatives – acknowledging the contribution each approach to ethics has to offer, and helping us behave in ways that maximise the positive consequences of what we do within the bounds of what we believe our moral responsibilities to be.

If this sounds daunting or complicated, it need not be so. A simple, practical way of setting our moral compass is to address the following questions when making a decision:

- Are there particular rights, values or duties towards others that are relevant in the situation?
- Are any of these moral absolutes which should outweigh all other considerations?

- What are the likely consequences of taking a decision?
- What is the virtuous thing to do?

This approach does not necessarily mean that those facing the same issue will come up with the same answer or make the same choice, but it does mean that we are approaching our decision-making in an informed way in which we can allow our principles to come to bear. In doing so, we will have addressed with some rigour Margaret Silf's fourth test of narrowing-down choices: how do they sit with our conscience?

FOR REFLECTION
Think of an ethical decision you have made recently. What factors did you consider in making your decision?

13
Ethics and Consumer Choice

ONE WAY IN which we can put our ethics into practice is as consumers. In a study of global markets, Albino Barrera, who is a professor of both economics and theology, provides a fascinating yet disturbing insight into how we can be inadvertently complicit in causing suffering to many of the world's poorest people because of our choices as consumers.[7] One way we can respond to this is by allowing ethics to inform the choices we make when shopping.

Using the sort of reasoning advocated in the previous chapter we may decide, for instance, that:

- Reducing global poverty is a moral imperative.
- Compassion and generosity towards others are virtues we wish to cultivate and apply as consumers.
- We are aware that the consequences of buying goods that we know are produced in sweat-shops by those who are poorly paid and mistreated is more likely to reinforce rather than relieve their situation.

---

[7] Albino Barrera, *Market Complicity and Christian Ethics*, (Cambridge: Cambridge University Press, 2011).

Using this sort of reasoning may sound as if it is likely to cause more problems of the kind addressed earlier on: making decisions about choice more difficult, involving more research. Given the increasing complexity of choice, sometimes it is tempting to lay aside our principles, justifying our actions on the grounds that in the global market they are inconsequential and will have no impact. However, a fundamental principle of Christian discipleship is that we should stick to our principles. Following Christ is never about taking the easy option for the sake of it. Furthermore, there are numerous examples of movements for social justice that have grown from almost nothing to create sufficient momentum to make a difference – and all because many people choose to do what they can, however small their action, for the common good.

A recent example of this is the success of Fair Trade, which depends upon consumer choice to make a difference on behalf of the world's poor. The principles of Fair Trade are clear: the producers are guaranteed a minimum wage and good working conditions, while consumers are prepared to pay a premium to ensure these objectives are met.

From very small beginnings, when the goods available consisted primarily of foods, beverages and craft products, and were sold mainly through charity shops and churches, Fair Trade has increased significantly in terms of both range and scale. A much wider choice of Fair Trade and other 'ethical' products are now available, including flowers and clothing, financial products, and even holidays to help the local economies in tourist destinations in developing countries. Fair Trade products are now to be found in supermarkets and high street shops, and are part of the mainstream.

One of the reasons why Fair Trade has been so successful is that it offers a practical, ongoing response to campaigns such as Band Aid, Live Aid, Make Poverty History and the United Nation's Millennium Campaign. Fair Trade also benefited from the unprecedented phase of economic stability and growth in many western countries which lasted until the dramatic financial crisis of 2007/8. Together, these helped generate almost exponential growth in sales of Fair Trade products.

Fair Trade has proved successful both in helping the producers involved, but also by sending signals through the markets that people should be treated fairly and with dignity. Fair Trade demonstrates that taking ethics seriously when making choices is worthwhile and can have impact – and the work done on behalf of consumers in terms of guaranteeing wages and working conditions removes the problem of researching choices. Ethical consumerism has been a lot easier as a result.

FOR REFLECTION
How might we, as consumers, make choices that benefit others as well as meet our own needs?

14
Choose Life!

WHEN THE ANCIENT Israelites were summoned together in the land of Moab having fled from slavery in Egypt, Moses offered them liberation in the Promised Land. The journey to the Promised Land was both a physical and spiritual one, and it involved making a choice: 'I call heaven and earth to witness against you today that I have set before you life and death, blessings and curses,' says Moses. 'Choose life so that you and your descendants may live'. (Deuteronomy 30:19).

This book is about choosing life – making choices that will help us and others to flourish. We have focused on two areas: coping with large amounts of choice, and making morally good choices. For the former, we have drawn on the research and insights of behavioural psychologists and others, for the latter we have looked at the Bible and the work of some of the great moral philosophers. Ultimately, however, it is up to us to put these and other insights into practice. The questions for reflection at the end of each chapter are intended to help in this process, by connecting the ideas explored in this book to the reality of our daily lives.

Choice is an issue that is receiving increasing attention because of its psychological effects. Interestingly, it was the subject of an article in the 2010 Christmas edition of *The Economist*, timed for the period when many of its readers were facing the annual dilemma of what presents to choose for their family and friends.[8] What hopefully distinguishes this book from such articles or other books on choice, or from self-help guides designed to help us cope with the complexities of contemporary life, is that it is first and foremost about Christian discipleship. Underlying all that has been written is a concern for how the choices we face from day to day relate to the 'better part' chosen by Mary and exemplified by Simon Peter.

A short book of this kind cannot explore the issues associated with choice in depth, but hopefully what it can do is highlight what the issues are and offer some guidance on how they can be addressed. The aim has been to offer suggestions for how to take an informed and disciplined approach to making choices, and to show how this can be developed in ways that not only help us to make good choices and not be overwhelmed by what we can choose from, but which becomes a practical expression of living a Christ-centred life.

On several occasions it has been noted that choice is intimately connected to freedom and the use of free will. The paradox of the need to contain or discipline how we exercise our free will if we are to use it to enable

---

[8] *The Economist*, December 18 2010, pp. 113-115.

ourselves and others to flourish has also been discussed. Christian discipleship involves taking a disciplined approach to life, not least in the way we use our freedom.

There remains one final and important thought to offer on the subject. At the beginning of this book, our diarist's entry ended as follows: *'Spend time thinking and praying about tomorrow – must decide whether to go to the church council meeting or a colleague's farewell party – should really be at both.'* For the Christian disciple, making choices is ultimately about bringing the options we face in our lives prayerfully before God, in the hope that 'God's will be done' through what we do. As we seek to grow closer to God, so we hope that day by day the lives we live may reflect God's will for us.

It is therefore appropriate to end with a prayer. The following, from the Prayer Book of the Anglican Church in Aotearoa, New Zealand and Polynesia, encapsulates so much of what this book is about and puts the choices we face into the context of Christian discipleship. It is, perhaps, a prayer we might turn to when making important choices.

> God our Creator, our centre, our friend,
> we thank you for our good life,
> for those who are dear to us,
> for our dead,
> and for all who have helped and influenced us.
> We thank you for the measure of freedom we have,

and the extent to which we control our lives;
and most of all we thank you for the faith that is
    in us,
for our awareness of you and our hope in you.
Keep us, we pray you, thankful and hopeful
and useful until our lives shall end. Amen.

15
Postscript: Religion and Rational Choice

MEMBERSHIP OF A church, or any other sort of religious affiliation, is a matter of personal choice – and increasingly so. One of the marked changes in religious life in Britain in recent decades is that there are fewer reasons to be part of an organised religion other than religious conviction. Going or gone are the days when upbringing, schooling or social convention would almost inevitably lead to involvement in church life at some level. Furthermore, today we are exposed to a wide range of faiths as well as strident atheism. It is increasingly the case that upbringing, education and society at large encourage us to make up our own minds about religion – including what religion (if any) to follow, and what tradition or denomination within a religion to join. We face increasing choice in the religious sphere just as we do in other aspects of life.

For someone exploring Christianity – or any other faith for that matter – the choices on offer can be confusing. No wonder people are tempted to be non-commital and say 'I'm spiritual, not religious.' It is beyond the scope of this book to defend the choice to be Christian, or to explore what is meant by 'Christian'

POSTSCRIPT: RELIGION AND RATIONAL CHOICE

given its varieties of expression. However, as a postscript to a book that has offered a religious reflection on a subject currently being studied by social scientists, it is worth noting that the relationship between choice and religion has also been something that has received attention in the social sciences.

'Rational choice theory' seeks to determine whether or not the choices we make are based on rational criteria, and is often used in economics to give insights into how we behave given the choices we face which have an economic dimension. Controversially, it has been put to use by sociologists to address the question: Is it rational to be religious?

Some social scientists take the view that using rational choice theory to study religion is not possible because religion is inherently irrational, based on unprovable tenets. Others argue that rational choice theory is not applicable to religion because religious behaviour cannot be analysed in the same way as, say, consumer behaviour. Others disagree, and in doing so argue that it is rational to choose to be religious because religion deals with deep and basic human needs and addresses fundamental questions: What is life all about? What are we here for? Where is it all leading to? What happens after death?

More controversially, however, the analysis is taken one stage further by some sociologists to argue that religion is rational because it seeks to 'reward' people by offering a response to these basic life questions through what they term 'compensators': people and institutions that compensate for the fact that we do not have all the answers. They help us address fundamental questions about the meaning of life and death. Churches, mosques, synagogues, temples, denominations, sects, priests – they are all 'compensators', to use the terminology. This view is controversial because it sees religion in terms of personal reward, rather than a spiritual quest or response to a sense of God's presence.

Another controversial point coming from this school of thought is that the greater the number and variety of these compensators in a society, the more people are able to find ways of addressing their deepest needs. Where there is a wide variety of religions on offer, so the argument goes, so there will be more 'vitality' to religious life. This is a surprising and optimistic view, as it is commonly thought that exposure to a wide range of religions can be unsettling and confusing rather than revitalising.

The British sociologist Steve Bruce, who is highly critical of the 'vitality' argument, takes a particularly pessimistic view of the effect of religious pluralism, and has written: 'This is the cancer of choice. To the extent to which we are free to choose our religion, religion cannot have the power and authority necessary to make it any more than a private leisure activity.'[9]

---

[9] Steve Bruce, *Choice and Religion: A Critique of Rational Choice*, (Oxford: Oxford University Press, 1999), p. 186.

POSTSCRIPT: RELIGION AND RATIONAL CHOICE

While organised religion may have lost much of its previous influence in public life and become more of a private matter, underlying this book is the conviction that Christian discipleship is far from being a 'leisure activity' or indeed a lifestyle choice: it is a matter of faith and personal conviction which unites many who share that conviction, albeit with different shades of understanding.

If religion is not to do with rewards and compensating for what we lack (as some sociologists argue), it may nevertheless offer a response to the human desire for order and meaning. Perhaps one reason why people find religion helpful is that they perceive it to offer structure and guidance for the way we live our lives. If this book in some way serves the purpose of helping those who choose to follow Christ to deal rationally with the complexities of choice they face, by giving some structure and guidance to making choices, then it will have served its purpose.

Suggestions for Further Reading

Michael Allingham, *Choice Theory: A Very Short Introduction* (Oxford: Oxford University Press, 2002).

Neil Messer, *Christian Ethics* (London, SCM, 2006).

Barry Schwartz, *The Paradox of Choice: Why Less is More* (New York: Ecco, 2004).

Margaret Silf, *On Making Choices* (Oxford: Lion, 2004).

DARTON·LONGMAN + TODD

Also in the *Simple Faith* series

FAITH
Margaret Silf

'Simple faith is simply to journey in trust, like a baby, but with the wounds and scars of an adult, like a man who died on a cross, and invites us to "become like little children", and when we follow him we discover that his footsteps lead right back, full circle, to a whole new beginning.'

A simple but profound exposition of the nature of faith in our contemporary world. In fifteen concise chapters Margaret Silf opens up searching questions, offers her insights, and invites the reader to think about his or her own responses. A gentle yet profound exploration of what we mean when we speak about 'faith'.

Order at www.dltbooks.com
or telephone
Norwich Books and Music on
01603 785925

DARTON·LONGMAN + TODD

Also in the *Simple Faith* series

FRIENDS
Clare Catford

'Friendship, whatever its shape, whoever it's with and wherever it manifests itself, is a divine gift.'

A funny and honest exploration of how to be a friend, both to oneself and others, how to keep the friends we have, and how to nurture friendships that may be difficult and challenging. In twelve concise chapters Clare Catford examines the complexity of friendships, including the necessity of befriending ourselves, and begins with the commandment that Jesus said was the most important of all: that we should love our neighbour as ourselves.

Order at www.dltbooks.com
or telephone
Norwich Books and Music on
01603 785925

DARTON·LONGMAN + TODD

Also in the *Simple Faith* series

HEALTH
Christopher Herbert

None of us can escape the pain and suffering of ill-health at times, and most of us will also at other times have to adopt the role of carer to loved ones who are sick. Such experiences bring into sharp focus our vulnerability, and can force some difficult questions to be asked, Why me? Why our family?

In this short book, Christopher Herbert explores these questions and the role of faith at such times, and seeks to offer support to all those who are struggling, be they patients or carers.

Order at www.dltbooks.com
or telephone
Norwich Books and Music on
01603 785925

DARTON LONGMAN + TODD

Also to come in the *Simple Faith* series in late 2012

MONEY

FAMILY

Order at www.dltbooks.com
or telephone
Norwich Books and Music on
01603 785925

DARTON · LONGMAN + TODD

THE OTHER SIDE OF CHAOS
Margaret Silf

'We will discover what new growth may be sprouting in our lives only if we risk the journey that takes us, like reluctant time travellers, hurtling through the uncharted universe of change.'

Your children have left home, you have lost your job, you have had to move to a strange town, your partner has died ....

Every life is filled with changes and transitions. In her new book, the popular writer and speaker Margaret Silf takes us on a journey through the pitfalls and the opportunities of change. Transitions may be awkward and uncomfortable, but they also put us into places where new life can flourish. *The Other Side of Chaos* invites us to embrace the inevitability of upheaval, and shows us how the leaving of our comfort zone can become an invitation to set ourselves free. Through stories and examples and down-to earth tips, we are helped and encouraged to live our transitions constructively and creatively.

Order at www.dltbooks.com
or telephone
Norwich Books and Music on
01603 785925